BY THE SAME AUTHOR

Collections
Languages
Exile
North of Nowhere
Iscariot's Dream
The Bone House
The Next Room
Ha Ha
White Lines
Mexico
Jackson's Corner
Mapland
Bridges
The Glass King

Pamphlets
Irish Notes (reprinted 2014)
The Farthest Circle
Mending Churches
Making Waves

Novels
Cillin
The Estate
Twenty Eight Worlds

Short Stories
Introductions 1

SOUR HILL

SOUR HILL

GARY ALLEN

Greenwich Exchange
London

Greenwich Exchange, London

First published in Great Britain in 2018
All rights reserved

Sour Hill © Gary Allen, 2018

Printed and bound by imprintdigital.net
Cover design by December Publications
Tel: 028 90286559

Greenwich Exchange Website: www.greenex.co.uk

Cataloguing in Publication Data is available from the British Library

Cover photo:

ISBN: 978-1-910996-24-9

CONTENTS

1/Prologue - In Search of the Narrator

2/The Narrator Puts One Foot in Front of the Other

3/The Builder

    The Workmen's Chorus

    The Chorus of Those Who Were Here Before

4/The Sex Carer

5/The Lovers

    The Shell

    Moon

    The Unknown Man

    Pig

6/Ghosts

    The Archaeologist

    The Skeleton Song

    The Man With the Black Beard

    Sligo

7/The Moravians

    Vikings

    Flax

    Moravians

8/The Nightwatch

    Blocks Within Blocks

    Green Men

9/Ferney

    Innerworld

    Inner World: Light

    Outer World

    Underworld

10/The Puppet Masters

    Hotel on a Frozen Beach

    The Mechanic

    The Dockers

11/Epilogue - The Poem Begins

1 PROLOGUE – IN SEARCH OF THE NARRATOR

What shall we say of him?
he was here for a short time
and then was gone
and who has really looked upon him?
who has stared into his face and can remember anything distinctive?
the people who have seen him without seeing him
can be counted like the days –
a thread of time that is of small measure
that is infinite.

We search him out, not because of what he has to say
but because he is actual in the small necessity of our story
but like the imagining of a ghost, he has become a ghost
and lost to us are the minuscule intimacies of his days on earth
the bored afternoons when he might or might not
have touched himself
the rainy walks among the swings
the insect histories of the hedgerows.

Give us war, we cry through boredom
or love, from a seedy sense of lustfulness
but the large Gods are as quiet as the stone Gods
the traffic Gods, the bedsit Gods
and the great metronome of the planets
shield our individual mediocrity.

Somewhere, in Sweden perhaps, a group of Saturday children
are shoving it out in a purpose built shopping mall
like children everywhere, but our narrator
is of one purpose, treading the one piece of earth
Sisyphus-like, on the sharp angle of a gradient
that is neither too steep nor too gentle
meeting no one that will remember him

for more than five seconds
and he knows it without thinking about it too much.

Take that lover, in the dark of a bedsit
he had her bent to his will
but it was as if his body belonged to someone else
and he was a puppeteer at the seaside
his mind moving over discarded underwear
as though trying to decipher the humanness of nature
like counting raindrops on the window
or the mantelpiece clock ticks
or the fine sand swirling on those seaside excursions
when he plashed about in the sewer water
that ran against history into a grey seminal sea
the studded cushion backs of a steam train
a Sunday school outing…

and then she was gone
washing between her legs, sitting on the toilet seat
and so our narrator was gone too
fading out of sense, like the desire to smoke an untipped cigarette
because he felt he had to
like he had to walk this hill again and again
as if he was a homosexual in a concentration camp
finding solace in the nakedness of his fellow workers.

Sour Hill? Why Sour Hill?
stupid bourgeois name
stupid bastardised Irish name
for a clump of ground that no one will fight over
like a seed that has gone astray
and grows annoyingly somewhere in the collective mind.

2 THE NARRATOR PUTS ONE FOOT IN FRONT OF THE OTHER

Nothing needs to be done, everything happens anyway –
if I stopped climbing this hill
if I stopped descending this hill, Sisyphus-like
and sat for a moment, on this wet ground
by the gated entrance to this evangelical church
my existence would go on regardless.
I am in a kind of space suit that has five senses
that connects me to the physical world
that connects me to other people
and by that same reasoning, I can close myself up like a seed
and what can be seen from windows
from cars, from whatever is passing,
is not, in a sense, me
but a form, a shape shifter, a moment of reflection
going from A to B on the Sour Hill Road.
That this is nightshift, is another story
like all the stories I carry within
and digest, or swallow, or suppress
so that I become blind, deaf, and dumb
like a man who is at the end stage of his multiple sclerosis
how else to deal with the boredom that life has become?
I have watched others slow to such a degree
as to become somnolent in life
like slow rain slipping off a pine branch –
you have to stare unblinking to catch it fall.
Now that I am dead as such
now that I am comatose
I can forget my history
the places I have travelled
the human experiences I have hated or applauded
the books I have written for my own understanding

like a hill, like a name place
a townland, a geographical Royal nonesuch –
at least for a fourteen hour shift.

3 THE BUILDER

One million red bricks, an estimate
cooling towers, chimneys, power points
dry risers, basements, wet risers
water points, windows, doors internal
/external, floors, concrete heads
steel/iron girders, L slope designs
firewalls, open plan, landscaped gardens.

Before, there was only fields and wasteland
but I had a vision, I had a dream, what laymen saw
as misguided visions of beauty and nature
I saw something more beauteous –
a building, rising from cleared land and muck
day after day, week after week, month after month
rising out of the ground by the truck load
simple man coming together with simple man
to put my plan into creation –

I am not a nobody, I am not nothing –
from early childhood, I knew I wanted to build –
high school, university, marriage
were only vehicles to my goal
and when I am gone, others will pass through the door
to work here in purpose-built surroundings –
my eyes watching them from every brick and fixing –

the walkways and ramps, the fountains
the lawns and car parks and network
of drains and gullies and suspended ceilings
and yes, some will even die here
aneurysms in the ground floor toilets
easy ambulance accessess
easy cleaned floors and walls
so, that as we come here, we leave
and might never have been.

The Workmen's Chorus

The overtime was great
like the playing-cards, the builder's tea,
the chemical toilets, the pounding noise
of overhead cranes, and jibs, and swinging girders
of angle grinders, and cement mixers
and fag ends, of plasterers and brickies
and carpenters, and electricians, and plumbers
and painters – but we came first

forget your planners and architects
and designers and engineers
hands like shovels, we navvied the earth
bending it to our will, and all the silly sods
who will sit behind computers
and give their lilywhite husbands neurotic blowjobs

what became of us? stopped one evening
coming home from a site –
they lined us up on a greasy country road
whose name I never knew then or now
and took the only Catholic to the side
who pleaded for us like Job
but they riddled us, men and boys,

with machine guns anyway
and as we lay dying, they laughed and finished the job –
and now I am nowhere, revisiting again and again
this stretch of winter road.

The Chorus of Those Who Were Here Before

Time needs walls to house in memories –
that everything changes, but ourselves
who are without form
as shiftless shapes scrape out the landscape
for centuries that have no meaning

as clouds glance the sky
birds fly, reflections on water
seasons blow like bog heather
round the compass of our eyes

aware always of each other's presence
but unable to touch, or smell, or see
buildings rise like summer flowers
to fall again, people walk like absurd apparitions
seen in quick duplications in shop-windows
and are gone, but we remain, rooted
like the crows in the dying woods
unable to pierce the film that separates you from us.

4 THE SEX-CARER

We are inside our bodies
travelling through this life
and it is through our bodies that we understand
the physical world around us
in touch, smell, and pleasure, we communicate

my body in the mirror is voluptuous
my breasts are large and vein-lined
my body is middle-aged –

once, in a younger self, I would have hated my form
the varicose veins, the broken nails
the thinning hair, the discoloured skin
the way my sex has fallen

but now I have learned to accept myself
a body impregnated with years of life
and sex is not just for the beautiful
and sex is not just about getting your oats
but is a beautiful way to express ourselves in this existence

and no one is deformed or ugly
and no one should be denied this form of love.

In my little two room, ground floor apartment
with my books on spiritual massage and Buddha
my incense and oils and diplomas
from little-known European universities
with the appraisal of small-town professors –
I reach out to the hurt in this world.

Take poor Benny, blind, deaf, and without speech
at first he was violent

lashing out at the physical world he couldn't comprehend
he would stand in the room and urinate
it took a long time to gain his trust
petting and stroking and showing him
how to bring himself to orgasm
sometimes we would just lie in warm water
sometimes he would smile
and then I knew I had reached him

or John, who had Down's syndrome –
we would meet three times a month
and I would bring him to orgasm with my hand
he thinks I am his girlfriend
he tells everyone I am his girlfriend
though I try to explain to him I am not

or Joe, a mature man with brain damage
he can fly into a rage
so we lie naked on his bed together
he is the only one I kiss
I touch and stroke until he comes
and I know he is so grateful

and Paul, a damaged young man –
his father remains silent when I am there
so that I think he doesn't want me there
but he always pays upfront
and waits in the other room
while I masturbate his son
and then he asks me,
How do you know he likes it?
How can you be sure?
Isn't it a form of abuse?

which makes me mad
for then I have to explain it all over again
and he listens, sighs, and says,
'OK, next month again?'

The wife is a different kettle of fish
we meet up as friends
sit in her kitchen and drink coffee with cookies
we talk about everything so naturally
about books, Buddhism, spirituality
her marriage, about the pain
and guilt she feels over Paul
about my early prostitution
and what brought me to this backward country –
we have become friends

so that, when he died
we comforted one another and kissed.

There is one man whom I visit
who is at end-stage multiple sclerosis
I have known him for a long time
he is the only one I have fucked
but he was so gentle and respectful
so quiet in his being
he showed me his books of poems
it was like fucking with a lover
something I hadn't felt for a long time –

and then he died, I went to the funeral
to celebrate his life and the part of me
that I liked to think will remain with him
in his body's death.

At night, I listen to the trees
as they blow and sway out across the fields —
they remind me of the voices
of all the damaged men I have touched.
I have a young blond lover
from Eastern Germany
we fuck like crazy teenagers
until it hurts

he tells me the Mexican Goddess Coatlicue
is a fearsome divinity
a skirt of snakes
decapitated heads hanging from her belt
the red mouth of her sex
has the power to attract and silence men.

5 THE LOVERS

The Shell

We are in a dream of our own making
or, at least, our connivance
where the physical is felt and seen
as through a mechanical process –
and no one can reach us
and no one can tell us what is real
what trees or the sky or the sun
the day, the night, looks like
how within the velvet nothingness of being
we echo emptily like a hollow cave.

There are many names
and just because we are unable
to use spoken language
we may be more aware than we appear to be
extremely sensitive – crowds
bright lights, noise, can be overwhelming
self-injury, my only contact
is the feel of my head banging
against the stubbornness of walls
or ripping the hair bloody from my scalp
the sleeplessness, the violent fits
the sea-pull of my moods –

and then someone reaches me from outside
somehow different, the smell of incense
the soft breath and touch upon what I sense
what you outside would call a body

and everything moves in conjunction
until the warmth engulfs me, and I cry out.
Don't ask me if I like or dislike it –
I have no knowledge beyond the blind centre
of my world.

Moon

I live in a flat
I look out at cars
I live with other people who shout at me
for messing-up the kitchen

sometimes my carers will visit me and talk
some I like, others make me cross

I have a job in a day-care centre
where I make things with others

and I have a girlfriend
who comes to see me once a month

and I lie naked on my bed
and she tickles me
and she touches me
and I touch her
large breasts, between her legs
and then she pulls me off
mostly I like it when the stuff comes out
but sometimes I get angry
and slam doors.

She says she is not my girlfriend
but what else is she if not?
Why do we do these things together?

Sometimes I get lost on the street
and the houses all look the same
when this happens, I sit down on the pavement
and I cry and cry and cry.

The Unknown Man

What is death? the loss of pain
the sudden drop in temperature
behind the wall cavity
separating this world from the next

or the rush of time
forward, backward
beyond the headstones and the square of blue sky

the iron gates, the faces I recognise
but can't quite place.

Strip down these wires
burn off the myelin sheaves
until I am a child again
delighting in poetry
putting plastic bricks on top
of brightly coloured plastic bricks

throwing bread to the migrating ducks
on the park dam
with an aunt in the wooden shelter
who is somewhere out there
with the others who have gone.

Or is death denial? Not being able to accept
the situation you find yourself in –
just like in life:

then she came round that last time
before it was too late
and laid me gently on the floor
undressed me and herself
and she smiled without speaking
as she placed her naked body on top of me
and put me inside her
so that I cried, like a thing that was dying.
And the walls, and the clock
and the books, and the rain on the window
slowly dissolved into themselves like candle wax.

Pig

She is slovenly, doesn't shave away the coarse hair
and she farts, and picks her nose
and her toenails are crumbling
under the colour red

she never makes over the bed
and drinks throughout the day
the car floor littered with chocolate wrappers
and crumbs and condoms and tubes of lubricant

if I want money, I have to steal it from her purse
if I want love, I have to grind it out
between her fat cellulite thighs
she teases me, 'Are you jealous of my work?'
but it turns me on, for now.

In the morning, when she is gone
I become a shell
conscious in her bed, that I have nothing
that I have nowhere to go
that I am not a Buddhist
that I am not religious
that this is not my country
that I know no one but Coatlicue
the Goddess of snakes and death
fearful to look upon
devourer of the weak:

and I see a wasteland of factories
and farmland covered in dirty snow
where a long black sooty train
scatters crows under a blue sky
and the trees are stunted
and the iron barns are oxidised red

and my father holds up a pig's head
still dripping, and strangely human
now that it is without life,
and laughs,

Look little Pete, your stillborn brother.

6 GHOSTS

The Archaeologist

Sometime, in the eighteen-hundreds
a local amateur archaeologist
was digging and destroying cairns, dolmens, burial sites
thinking he was throwing light on ancient times
when actually he was obliterating the past

when he unearthed the remains of some seventy skeletons
men, women, and children of different ages
and all seemingly from the same period
and all seemingly had met a violent death –

the skulls were stoned-in, or had large triangular stones
lodged forcefully into their mouths
and the legs and arms were twisted out of shape
as if to stop them rising and walking among the living

ancient Celts? Vikings? we are still not sure
but certainly ritual, and certainly very painful deaths.

Our archaeologist misfit friend
was quickly ousted from the find
and contented himself with seeing out his days
keeping seven beehives for honey
until he died in the middle of the night
apraxia with too much good living

and found himself fully aware in death
though he didn't know he was dead
and as much a part of the past as the past
he helped to destroy

walking out in a perpetual misty night
along the field lanes and byways of Sour Hill
though most of them have been concreted over
built upon, and sometimes, he can be seen
walking through walls
and waving his hands
as though he were pushing aside branches
or warding off evil.

The Skeleton Song

We were human just like you
we drank, and ate, and argued
and fucked our way from hut to hut
and washed off lice from braided hair
and killed, and suffered as you still do

imagine, the actuality of stone
solid impact forced into your mouth
until the jaw bones crack and lock
or your limbs smashed like extracting marrow
and twisted from the sockets to rest
around your neck

laid in the cold ground, foot to foot
and buried alive, the living world
receding through the one eye
of a little piece of blue

and yes, it's true, I would have shouted louder than the rest
would have smashed your jaws apart
to live a little longer

we all worship something
in the earth or sky or sea or ground
false Gods are only evil to those who pray to something else
while others die and rise and walk about
we are pinioned to this plot of soil
unable in our ghostly forms
to talk or move. Amen.

The Man with the Black Beard

They see me running quickly to my meeting place
a stooped man, of small stature
with a black beard, and black hooded cloak
quickly running through the work's canteen
to my meeting down by the river field
the ghostly shapes of night time hay stooks
the noisy weeded water
the confounded cawing of rooks in the swaying trees
I'm always running to meet him –
this is my eternity –
the gentleman who deals out souls
who plays upon your conceit:

everything is shades and shadows to me now
I no longer feel amazed or confused

it's all just another form and play of damnation
these people at the drinking cooler
who stop and stare
that farmer coming home late across the fields
those idiots who cross themselves and spit
who don't realise that God has no time for us here.

In my room, I played the cards
thought myself clever to a fault
above the peasants and the chains of the earth
my shadow became a rook
a bird of prey, a hawk
I flew on invisible wings over the squares of fields
the huts, the middens, the meeting houses

and felt myself a thing apart
from lowly man or God
until the darkness that floods the heart
and cries to me across the endlessness of time.

Sligo

In my life, everything has become strange
to me, yet familiar: the time of the morning star
is the same, the lowing of cattle in the byre
the rooks waking in the trees
yet, once, I could reach out and touch walls…
this great house echoes with the sleeping
this great house, like a hollow heart
empty, paper dry, ethereal

the stone walls, dry ditches, small loughs
sea and wind and hovels of Sligo are gone
my Catholic faith is gone

seventeen hungry mouths
some that never lived beyond infancy
are gone, so they sent me up North
away from my own customs and people
up here, among the gentry and the heathen
that I might live, of sorts
and the house-keeper is dry like gin
and the other servants rigid like sticks
and the gentry might sit on the right of God or Devil
but we look to the ground when they walk past

and the cook is a fat Presbyterian who hates me
and piles job upon job, thinks me stupid
that I don't talk right – what else would I do?
I may as well hail from a foreign country
on my half day off once a month
the stone faced town's people scratch their heads and stare
neither making head or tail of my papish tongue

so I lay with him in the tall grass down by the river
the way I had seen my parents
when they thought we were sleeping
the way animals mounted each other
and stuck it in – I no longer
remember his Protestant face
the farm lad, who thought he
had the better of me
with his talk and coaxing
and his quick rut:

but I remember pain like a sudden cloud
the emptiness of the soul
the burning pain in my legs and arms
as I scrubbed the fire bricks
inside the great fireplace

the procession as they carried me delirious
up the small top staircase
to the shuttered bell tower folly
and the narrow cot they laid me on to die
too tight and frightened to fetch a doctor

and, like a lamp turning on and off
the menagerie of faces and shutters
opening and closing, and through days
of wind and cloud and rain
and a boy's thin cock in my hand
in a field of grass and insects and games.

Then confusion, the feeling that I am, somehow,
absent, that days and nights no longer matter
that my mind has spaces that can't be filled
yet the routine of walking from the maid's room
on the top floor
to the kitchen and seeing these strangers as lost as me
and sometimes they might stare back
as if seeing me
a materialisation of sorts

winter days have light in them
is hard to define –
we could be up among the tight clouds
or face down on the hard ground
that smells of sleeping potatoes or wheat

and here by the coke vending machine
the light turns to thick grey
and something struggles to come into being
inhuman, but with a life of its own
human shaped, but not of flesh or blood
that stays for a moment in its own eternity

and then is gone
as though the struggle was too great.

Night time brings its own definition –
green luminescent lights show the way
from floor to floor, and doors and lift shafts
creak on their own timescale
like empty wheelchairs
spiralling out of control down steps
like Chinese whispers in the dark corners
or family photos on desks facing one another
with burning anonymity
or plastic wall clocks breathing quietly
like pacemaker hearts
caught suddenly by the moon

whose faces all become human for a moment
and become the man who broke
every bone in his feet
by being blown off a seaside cliff
or whose heart exploded like a small bomb
and flung him through
the country post office plate glass window.

Only the alcoholic or the loner
would stick these shifts
never speaking to one another
of the slamming doors
or the fleeting shadows in the basement or canteen
the lady who suddenly appears smiling
by your left shoulder
and is gone
leaving you like a paper-dry leaf
oscillating between spider webs.

What is death and dying?
the repeat performance of a book or a generation?
or the calendar of histories?
the sudden awareness of existence
and the cringing understanding,
that the routine has a stopping mechanism
where the block falls quicker than an eye-shut
and then there is nothing,
or something,
or both.

7 THE MORAVIANS

Vikings

One gold torque he found
in the alluvial soil of the river hinterland
as though someone had cast it carelessly aside
either in drunkenness, or battle, or murder
or while lying with a local daughter or wife:

a hard clear night, even for an Irish summer
the moon blunted by the fog
as if lost in this branch of waterways
the wooden punts and leathered oars
navigated this river system

the cold eyes, the cold metal
of helmet, chain, and sword
fell like an eagle's talons
among the mud and straw

and dragging the monks away from the altar
disfiguring them in the pursuit of gold
raping some of the younger men

the only sound of life that makes life real
like a cleansing, the screams
the crackle of wood and straw and fire
the slaughter and noise of beast and man alike
from this dung heap to the coasts of Greenland

and when they were gone, after seven days
they came out of hiding, from the woods
and the sacred groves, the hollow mouths
carved into stones and trees
from the smouldering fields, to bury the dead
to rebuild, and the monks told them
the way of sin is mortality and death,
they had visited this hell upon themselves.

But what has changed? In this landscape of the soul?
hiding in bedrooms with slat blinds
caught in the slow fire of satellite television
laptops, iPhones, or flesh on high-definition screens
we sleepwalk towards an eternity of doom
the willing victims of an outside world
that is greater than our comprehension
the round towers that have become minarets
the stink of heavy oil and blunt knives
even now, there are men being whipped for kneeling to pray in the
wrong way

and through the walls we sense the fear
that lies beyond a river bend
a copse of trees, a gentle hill
and fields, the housing estates

the government and commercial buildings
that are as unreal in the dark
as a sword in the belly
or a heavy axe cleaving the soul.

Flax

We shall call him Allen, stealer of sheep on the borders
A reaver, but he could be anyone
little men of field work
little artisans of iron or wood or weaving
they thought they were big men with universal ideas
of comradeship and freedom and enlightenment
and built themselves a high stage
like a gallows platform
on which to dangle from history

and rot, like the sweet heavy flax
in the stagnant weedy water:
forty strokes took the skin from Allen's famine back
for pulling the pike from the thatch
and marching like a green fool
along country lanes that seemed giant with familiarity
and would see bicycles and cars
at roadblocks in the dead of night
and men like Allen wired tight to milk churn bombs
and men like Allen, who thought they were big men
in their own eye motes
as they booby-trapped gullies and culverts
and broke apart bone like tree splinters
while cowards slavered under blankets
dreaming of lottery wins, the young girl next door.

And everyone beats drums
and pushes hay wagons
against the Meeting House doors
and sail off skulking to Carolina or Kentucky
to nurse festering sores:

on this hill I was held captive
with the local milkman who looked strange with fear
but it didn't seem real, as they set-up the ambush
of a local part-time soldier.

I suddenly took flight, and ran downhill
like a great clumsy bird
through thick undergrowth
to the light in the window of a farmhouse
belonging to one I knew well
who, I supposed, would be dressed and at breakfast
getting ready to milk his small herd
like he did every ordinary morning
for some hundreds of years

and I heard the milkman shout my strange name
as a bullet, or maybe more, came whistling close like wind
but my legs kept propelling me forward

and he opened the door and looked at me
as though I were mad
or the dead risen
a scowl that said I shouldn't visit
such things upon the simple living.

Moravians

Late Autumn is the time when everything languishes
it is all time-encased
the time of your parents and grandparents
and all your ancestors are unchanged

the nights and mornings are dark
the day span dull
time is judged by the sound of crows
against the morning sky and early moon:

the alien saucer-shaped spaceship
is actually a modern church in an old country
the thin metal spire represents the cross
the heavy gates and cattle grid
the corrugated roofs of the tea rooms
the Sunday school and youth club
are lead coloured
against the natural colours of the extant volcano –

if Christ came back, he wouldn't understand this Christianity
the Jerusalem Pilgrim is a liar and a whore
in her best Sunday hat and floral dress
designer handbag and middle-age exercise lessons
the half-wit from down the road
with his petit mal and giant bible
groping the young girls between the legs
the maintenance fitter, born again,
driving the Sunday School bus with one eye in the mirror
watching the girls on the back seat
rubbing each other off

with their uncompromising politics
they praise God and split heads with umbrellas –

they are modern now
business flights to Amsterdam and Paris
conferences in community centres
in Texas, Stockholm, and Fermanagh

see how they dance and praise the Lord
like dervishes to Christian rock bands
those who served time for mutilating bodies
cutting throats, nailing limbs to public-house floors
drilling into knees and groins
now whisper about dark going-ons
in Iraq and Syria, where Christians
are crucified and beheaded –
send food-parcels and blankets and New Testaments

while down the road is Bethlehem
with its chapel and charity door
and bells, and gardens, and milking parlour
and the monk with one eye
who collects the milk bottles without speaking.

The lights are on early along the river path
balls of frost footstep the ground
if you stand long enough in the roadside bushes
you can hear the clang of harnesses
and the sound of hoofs and cart wheels:

the Moravian settlement sleeps four hundred years
the square houses of the single men and women
the meeting rooms, the functional graveyard on the hill
the patchwork quilt of tilled fields easy by the river
the patronage of the landowner
is all that stands between survival and superstition
while Cennick sings to them

from the dark forests of Moravia and Bohemia
and the little bookshop that sells its Christian pamphlets online
to America, Canada, and a woman from Berlin

for nothing has changed
the justified ending of a kill
the ways and means to gratify
the soul, anger, worship, or sin
the curtains closed on yesterday
and hold within the vacancy of our desires
of who round about is righteous or wrong
or getting more than we are.

This one lost among the chaff
reading his bible lessons after work in the Civil Service
pure of thought, no television
he makes-up a life of sin and shame
picking-up East European girls online
for lonely lunches in nature parks
promising more, they are bored
with packed lunches and feeding ducks
they turn to middle-aged men with respiratory problems
who don't want to die alone

or the petite oriental girl
like a night flower, who opens up
in the dark of a suburban garden
daring unsuspecting neighbours and passers-by
to see him as he really is
asking old men, do they want a smoke
from his painted full lips –
he never will, too frightened of the early morning knock
from the boys in uniform
the painful climb of courthouse steps
the cameras, the pointing

of one who came out, and paid the price
he sits lonely in his hire-purchase car
outside the apartments of Asian escort girls
too timid to go in and find out who he really is.

Evening time, despair, despair, despair
pointing fingers and sussing out
the frailty in others –

the kitchens smell of curry, spuds, or fries,
quiches, Indian, meat and veg
the old sit oddly at home with the new
the settled with the incomer

the television flat high-definition screens
that flicker just like analogue
behind the slatted or venetian blinds

as the frost and mist settles along this substitute Rhine
her little car parks like a heart thud
familiar yet strange
she lights her scented candles
prepares her odour rich oils
undresses her ample body as you undress
and lie down to her caresses
of parts that are diseased, numb
with no responses or autopilot function

and she gets you hard, does something she never did before
she takes you in, as you float in the cool water
beyond the bitterness of your tongue
the dark matter behind the eyes
the lesions of the myelin sheathes
the stripping down of electrical wires

where the curtains stood
and the walls, the cavities
the windows, the street
the open wallet on the side table
the hard nose of judgement.

8 THE NIGHTWATCH

Blocks Within Blocks

A giant hand might have gouged
out the land, and tore out the trees
and hedgerows, raked over the fields
and the good farmland, the cottages
the scrubland, even the sacred
hawthorn. And on what was left, they
built, these smiling faces from the
seventies, the brave new world
of architects and quantity
surveyors, structural consultants
clerks of works, building contractors
electrical contractors, mechanical
contractors, et al. Crawling like
ants over the erected steel rods
and cables, and table models, and
blue prints, these impossible
possible men, with their diverse
histories, consigned to history,
like all man's purposes, producing
over one thousand drawings.
Tragically killed in a motor

accident. Serving apprenticeships
as joiners. Reconstructing
textile mills destroyed during
the war. Bought this land
for twenty-one-thousand, six-hundred
pounds and a grinning sod
to cut the first sod and a naïve
fool for the inauguration. A
special luncheon, and a
commemorative drinking-fountain.
Grandstands and bunting and
tents and sandwiches and cups
of tea. A beautiful view was
planned and unrestricted by
buildings, so they left some
trees to augment the beauty
of man's handiwork, which,
all be told, has outdone nature
itself. Offices. Debating
chambers. Committee rooms.
Assembly hall, for conferences,
banquets, exhibitions, drama,
music, ballet, dancing, films:
a brave new world for the
locals, that perplexed the locals
who couldn't give a damn. Blocks
linked by vertical circulation
cores. A dining-room and
kitchen – what's not to like?
but for the homemade fertiliser
bomb packed into a Ford
Cortina, that blew the far
wing to pieces, while the young
woman kept the guards talking.
Never mind, the roof rising into

the air, and slamming back down,
or the red brick reduced to
red dust, or the hillock of
broken glass, all exposed
like the rib bones of a rotting
whale carcass. Never mind,
what we made, we can make
again, and the people enjoy
the landscaped gardens, the
ornamental fountains, the
unspoilt view of this master
-piece, of man's ingenuity.
Walk your Miniature Schnauzers
throw sticks, smell the flowers
and shrubbery, and the local
youths drink cheap cider
in the open grounds, smoke
dope, shag their girlfriends
roller-blade, cycle, skate
-board down the walkways
and the ramps, carve or
spray-paint the doorways
and brickwork. And tree saplings
grow on the flat roofs,
taking root in the dirt
and water on the asphalt,
like miniature Japanese
roof gardens in Tokyo
or New York, and the
roof of the great hall is
slowly caving-in under
its own weight, and the
crows wait nightly in
the branches of the trees, not
knowing anything of regeneration.

Green Men

If you stand in the almost dark
of the corridors outside the offices
or in the streetlight darkness of the
offices, you can hear the giant heart
of the building tick a regular pulse
like an office clock, in the black
veinways of the building, the only guide
are the green luminous men of
the exit signs above the doors
an eerie unearthly light, inhuman
like the men who walk towards them
killing time, being killed by time
followed closely by the unseen, unknown
an unfolded wheelchair pushed and
spiralling and toppling down the
corridor, followed by laughter
and footsteps, but, are they human?
At least they were human once
for everything that lives, or has
lived, is contained here as much
as in the vastness of the universe
the Milky Way, the galaxies, the black
holes of space, and time, and dimensions,
these good young men, fit for
nothing else in life, sent here
by the dole, for a pittance,
to this dead-end, like green
walking men, bringing in booze
and floosy girlfriends, fucking
on the sickroom beds, telling
ghost stories, breaking into
the cigarette machines, the canteen
freezers, spiralling out of

control on the night-air
rooftop, in the breeze, and the
town lights, and the stars, and
the great emptiness of everything,
courting dismissal and sniggering
disgrace – send me to the
chicken factory or the drug
den. Among those who watch
from the corners, the sluice rooms
the black shadows, the basement
boiler rooms and stores, and
grease traps, and inside risers,
are the recently departed who
finding themselves in transfiguration
shock, have nowhere else to go,
anchored to a perpetual recurrence
this one, like a thin rag of a
neurotic woman, pinched like an
old bird, old before her time,
spent the darkness of her
late evenings ringing everyone
she knew, waking them from
their sleep, cursing husbands,
crying children, the only lights
in the estate, to berate them
for their selfishness, their
disinterest, that a man had
passed her window, several
times in each direction, standing
under the street light with
his coat open, rubbing himself
and laughing at her – she
stopped calling, let them find me:
they followed the trail of notes
she left, out to the backyard

where they found her hanging
from a sorry looking tree, her slight
body twisting, the rope creaking,
her tongue black and protruding,
one arm a strange yellow
and the office colleagues asked
for a photo of the deceased
a piece of wood from the
tree she crucified herself
on. But she is not gone, raving
running rabbit-like down this warren
of corridors, stopping in
the headlights of the luminous
glow, before scowling and
running on, as if she had seen
the tall thin lady of the house
that stood here over a hundred
years ago, this cruel mistress
of the house, who walked at night
with a bunch of keys, and disappears
through the toilet walls, to the
maids' attic rooms, to catch
some slow girl up from the
country with not two pennies
to rub together, getting it doggy
style from the foot servant
old enough to be her father
with his yellow gassed lungs,
she scowls, and disappears
and turns a hostile eye to
watch the nightmen clock-on
for here they are, the Nightwatch
gathering in a Scottish pub
in Amsterdam, with their
swords and halberds and ribboned

sashes and amateur killing
looks – keys, torch, clocking
counter, faces tired and
palely white, not worth
tuppence, half-asleep, half
aware of their surroundings –
better than the chicken factory
the rows of sleeping turkeys,
if one gets distressed, they
all start flapping about and
shit all over you, listen, is
there someone in the yard,
where the rats keep close to the bins
and the walls, where the jays
and crows, and magpies
peck open the bin bags in the
skip, tossing out what they
can't eat, perhaps the
travellers are back again
breaking into the out-buildings
trying to steal the ride-on
lawnmowers, the tractors –
or maybe it's just the foxes
white socked, thin legs
elongated faces, or a couple
from the hotel dance, who have
found a secluded spot, away
from the lights – a doorway?
for a quick stand-up fuck, the sad
man watching from the darkness
of the other side of the window
masturbating at shadow images
the sound of water rushing in
the weir, where a man cracked
the bone of his skull open on

the iron sluice gates, and was
never in his right mind again
he hanged himself in shame
now walks the halls in
ghostly insomnia, making
phantom coffee for office
workers long gone, in lines
workmen in boiler suits or
bibs, who curse and spit and
tell dirty jokes, who play
Saturday morning league
and drink beer with
vodka chasers, who fight
and split lips, beat wives, have
hidden revolvers, know
people who can burn your
house – see how his frown
changes to a woman's smile
as he sticks his arse out
ladylike plays with the curled
hair on the back of their
thick necks, a lowly Charlus
these corridors and rooms
echo to the low groans of
their sweaty lovemaking
his ghostly eyes see a
lifetime's images in the
tunnel night-vision before
him, brass handles above
hotel beds in Brighton, the
flesh of beefy Irish navvies
under him, the noise that
makes him stop and stare
into the torchlight like a
grave robber or a blood sucker

or a parasite, and keeps on
repeating himself, like the
black beard who quickly
darts among the tables
and chairs, or the maid who
walks through the foyer walls
and disappears into the lift shaft
but who knows nothing of lifts
or anything from this world
but who is active, and still
alive in her own world, catching
strange glances now and then
of people and appliances that
have no meaning for her, the
old farmer at the desk, who
lost his dairy herd, who stinks
of the fish-farm he works
during the daylight hours, and
never changes his uniform
farting and eating the dried
husks from his own nose
the curled-up sandwiches
left outside committee rooms
hacked on and spat over
nibbled by mice, bluebottle
vomit, who has become a
beast like the animals
he neglected, he goes
outside and defecates
as if in a field
and worries that his Down's
syndrome daughter will marry
some money-grabbing Catholic cunt
when he is dead, after years
of putting shilling upon shilling

frauding the agriculture
ministry, gathering up paper
and tin cans, ten pounds a
ton, for money makes money
and life is hard, like frosty
mornings behind a cow's
rump, and if there are such
things as ghosts, what
does he care? Too dumb
to understand or give a damn
for the whole world is older and
more secretive than any
of us understands. There
are ones more ancient
who wait like old viruses
in the darkest of the shadows
who were there before
the architects, or the big
house, or the stone-fed skeletons
when the land was young
and who now watch with
wisdom's bemusement as
all the Nightwatch break
up into green luminous
dust and disappear like
streaks of ether into
the Perspex exit signs.

9 FERNEY

Innerworld

There was a white goat chained to an oak
in the centre of the garden of a big house
that seemed gigantic to me, being small and only a child
and the house itself didn't look like the other houses
but had stacks of tall chimneys and wooden shutters
on all the windows, and the goat had a beard
and dead stone eyes, like clear marbles
and it meant something more than a living lawnmower
it should have been on a shilling piece or something

and there was a long avenue of chestnuts
and a house with a clock set high into the gable
whose hands were always at the wrong time –
to fool the devil, and the pram kept catching
in the mud and stick ruts, so that I had to walk
and there was a monkey-puzzle tree
and balsa wood – where did it come from?
soft and rotten and light as a feather

whoever built the house, some general with a VC
from a small war in a far off land
where natives were mowed down
with maxim guns, like elephant grass
sowed the gardens and green-houses
with exotic plants and trees from all over the world
and during the big war, the GI's were stationed here
would bring up the local girls for dances and parties
dropping knickers for perfume and silks and cigarettes –

she would walk here in the winter afternoons
a young married woman with four children already

seeing death and old age as a small white chapel
on the distant hillside that seemed unreal among the fields
does any parent contemplate
the death they have passed on to their children?
even memory can't be trusted
for the sights and sounds and glimpses
that take us back for a moment to the past
are as meaningless as time present

the sound of that old motorcycle
in the yard, revving-up annoyingly
its frame rattling and spluttering
in diesel fumes and smoke
brings back my grandad
doing circles in the graveyard
scaring old women with flowers and prayer beads
like a bird feigning predators
away from a nest of eggs
he shooed them away from the caved-in crypt
where he had six Mausers in oil wrapping

or the classroom clear as window glass
when at last Ferney in goggles and trench coat
puttered kick-starting into the playground
an hour late

the dipsomaniac magician from somewhere in South Derry
with his coloured handkerchiefs
white balls and disappointment
who lost the last of his ambition
down the torn lining of a child's school blazer.

And even farther back, the tobacco
and rancid fat stink
of a council house, the bay window

where the pram sat, behind the settee
where the quick shock of sunlight
reflected in an open window
of a car mirror, caught the eye
in wonderment, through the drone
of adult voices I couldn't recognise
individually yet, and the violet colour
shower of dancing dust motes:

I am certain life and death are one and the same
circles that gather quickly to a centre
then expand outward again
that the GI's are still highballing all over Europe
my grandfather greasing rifles
sad old Ferney getting tricks
all fucked-up and hating his audience of Protestant children
nipping from a hip-flask and forgetting
where he had come in, or how far into a trick

and still out there, gravitating towards a centre
where we all meet and understand what it is to suffer
in another existence

on Sour Hill, they took me to the cottage
of an old man in tartan who played lively on a fiddle –
was he related to me?
like the uncle who swarm like a swan
to Sydney, and died a bus-conductor
never having married or written home
or those other uncles, aunts, and cousins
who coming once into sharp focus
speak once, and fade out into rows
of teachers, and shop assistants, and school friends
the legions of the dead who listen fleetingly to fiddle music
like heavy rain upon dusty rhododendron bushes

like slow water running into the park dam
from a culverted stream
that ran under the road and houses
the latticed batten fences
the manicured hills
and flower beds and tennis courts
and the statue of Armed Science
and the bloated bodies fouled
with muck and flies and shit
of dogs and ducks and birds
carried into the sewage overflow
where, to keep us away from daring each other
to walk around the narrow rim,
they told us that it was the devil's cup
a hole to the centre of the earth
a gateway to hell, but hell was in front of us,

to me now, was the convex
mirror of the lake, where the cold blue sky
and the depot, and the Cottage Hospital where children were born
curved round like the glass dome
of a snow shaker
making the earth I walk upon an ancient heaven
the sky a hell in a child's memory.

Inner World: Light

Light. Everywhere, light.
Like camp fires, spotlights, theatrical lights
that blind my eyes, that dazzle
with a burning confusion behind the eyes
as though burned into the medulla of the brain
a kaleidoscope of light and sound
that could be the years spinning out of control
down the interior of memory:

there is music, coming from somewhere
outside the darkened room
a jumble of adult voices, laughter, and shouting
drunken voices, ghostly babble
from the antiquated barrack
buildings behind the recently
placed curls of barbed wire
and the rain-blurred security lights

as I sat in the pitch-black back bedroom
threw open the musty curtains
on the yard's dog-barking pretence at silence
and wondered, were they there?
among the beehive hair-dos and crew-cuts
the outlying hills that could have been
the sand hills of Aden or Suez

and the door handle to the room missing
the stolen pub ashtrays and broken fob watches
beside his bed, the sounds of a body
terrified, out of its surroundings
like family bibles and pocket-books
and dusty Christmas decorations
and demon faces engrained on wardrobes and drawers.

The town lights at the end of the badly lit street
the wet pavements, the walls of the old cemetery
where corpses lie and fall in upon themselves
yet must have walked here, or ran
like a small boy to McKenna's on a Saturday night
pretending he is a train, or the Pony Express
dazzling drunks, jumping puddles of vomit
vaguely aware that his father
is a man in a faded second hand post-office suit
going bald, a double chin

a neck scarred with lanced boils
a packet of Woodbines
that his father is out there too

or the blue and red and yellow lights
of the gas-works
on a dark afternoon
the steel hoops of the bridge
and the pawn shop of useless things
too old and done and broken to haggle over
but the radio, and the old men's hushed talk
and the smell of familiarity of a generation for sale.

And my mother was out of her depths
a small freckled girl
who had vague principles of right and wrong
of family loyalty and social morality
who had nothing against Catholics, but
when the blood is up!
who spotted a small plane
above the factories and mills and fields
on the Sunday war was declared
on the great wooden radio that sat
like an old Testament God on its own bracket
high on the wall, its foreign voice
mumbling truisms all across a backward Europe
and the old people in their hovels
who, although poor and of no importance
to men in moustaches and jodhpurs
thought they were going to be beaten and die
and she lay in the long grass looking up
and wondered if a small bomb would be dropped
over the side, she didn't care
not even for the soil on her Sunday frock –
nothing, as always, happened

she knew nothing of the man
who was twelve years older
who had walked out of the spinning-mill to join-up
for the fun of it, to get away
to prove himself on a world stage
who would be gathered up
and swept away with millions of others
by an indifferent world
among the pine trees of Sour Hill
or Katyn, or the desert of frozen fields.

And I see him again, after years
of stunted growth
in a demanding child's eye
reflected in shop windows
going down the stairs of subways or bargain stores
where the struggle to make ends meet
became a lifetime of heroic mediocrity.

They were neither film stars
nor famous, nor important, nor had basically different experiences
from anyone else
nor unique in a random world
of stupefying sex and birth and dying.

And the boy huddled with fear in the back bedroom
on a Saturday night
trying to recall some scrap
of his Sunday catechisms
will always be there
a malevolent marker on their
lives and movements
a judgement on their thoughts
hidden even from each other
in the deeper subconscious of the mind

like each parent having a difficult birth
in the forests and mountains and borders of an Austria.

Outer World

And all at once you are rushing headlong into the future
that is no longer the future but a moment frozen in time
that comes again suddenly into your consciousness –
a bright warm Saturday evening out from The Hook
the fields flat and stitched with ditches and canals
the door of the connecting corridor
open to the sunlight and the rushing air
the stately homes and silver poplars
the stations and shimmering car bonnets
the railway cuttings and still water
the mad houses and austere churches
and the flat you left back there littered with unused condoms
sharing a bottle of Jenever with
a dark skinned girl who would later
sell herself on the open market
and go insane, or was always insane,
shutting herself away in sparse rooms
sucking-off the older male patients
and seeing the dead everywhere
at every window and street corner
screaming at shadows
defecating in the hallways of sheltered accommodation
the long wait, the endless Saturday waits
drinking beer with Dutch girls
in a country pub among the forests of Luxemburg
eating cold tomato soup in a bar
up an alleyway on the Mariahilfer Strabe
in Vienna, trying to retrieve a shoe
from the yard of a pension in Baiersbronn

and listening to a radio giving the German football results
reading month-old newspapers
with down and outs in a station yard
in a backwater in Italy and stealing
Lira tips from the restaurant counter
all becomes one, without individual representation
and there is no glory or achievement
in sinking to the bottom
of finding the base human ingenuity
to deceive and use and move on without guilt.
The immigrants of Amsterdam
(or Europe for that matter)
are uncorrupted by our feeble European ways
they bring with them their own desert patience
preying in the station concourses
for naïve Western meat
weaving the silk threads of deception
until they have them in one room apartments
out by the ring roads, autobahns, railway lines
knocking them about, children, grandparents
who listen from the next room
as they fuck and fight and realise
they are miles apart.
And it is easy to buy anything in Amsterdam
it is easy to buy qualifications
to teach English to special needs children
or immigrants. How I love
the multi-coloured women in their little boxes
trading insults, and phone cards and H
flashing worn out tits and child-bearing stomachs
for the desperate men who stand in the dark
and who feel cheated by how little is in return
while history melts around the blurred lights
of the canals, gold gilt on church towers
and monuments wilt with the whirling lights

of ambulances and police cars.
And once I joined a self-defence force
carrying nightly around the housing estate
a Luger my father brought back from Germany
after the war – it would have blown up in my face
if ever I had the guts to fire it
and anyway, the firing-pin had probably been filed away
though we did fire-bomb Hassan's taxi depot
ran from the front room of a terraced house
I never did understand why
but my mother saw soldiers in every street
and told me to run from Ireland
only to find that every street was the same
that all the women were just as hungry
and everyone hates what they can't conceive
children like piglets sleeping in one bed
under damp blankets and the disappearing
or concealed things we grow up with –
ringworm, lice, fleas
the shame of adolescents
the body changing and demanding gratification
with no thought or knowledge of love
but the quick animal thrusting
into another's body and humiliation
almost as shameful as red exercise books
scribbled with childish writing
that were called poems
words misspelled and laughed at
caught helpless in a net of creation
like a mad girl broken open by a line of men
dulled by their own senseless rhythms
going home to their wives with the evening papers
whose headlines dance in the dim lighting
forty years from now
until you find your life has passed

like soapy blood down a drain
and has been meaningless in an uneventful way
that to get from A to B
could have been accomplished in a straighter fashion
that one set of female sexual organs
are just as seductive as many
and all the chimneys of the suburban houses
are firing out sparks and orange flame
the Halloween All Souls evening tangible on your tongue
the roundabout way to return home
Ulysses like, to find, that in reality,
you were only another production-line Sisyphus
groomed and indented and prejudiced
just like all the rest
books of poems out of print
the space winds of the Troubles
moved on to the Middle East and Africa
and somnolent, you find a room
a place to hide, a hill
to walk up and down, hoping some young woman
will take you aside
into the darkness of the moist hedgerows
away from the luminous street lights
and put her mouth on yours
reach into your trousers
like in the films you saw
like in the books you read
like when you were young and uncorrupted.

Underworld

It is Saturday afternoon again:
is it Saturday afternoon again?
Really? There is a vagueness in the air
if you will, there is a feeling deep inside me

that questions everything many times over
like a tramp on stage
so that I am fatigued with questions and answers

it is Saturday – is it? – it is Saturday afternoon
even if time and dimensions have no meaning anymore
the street lights are on
the televisions are flickering
the chimneys are smoking
though chimneys don't smoke anymore
I am in an apartment overlooking Stanley Park
in Vancouver? no, I am in the Dakota Building
overlooking Central Park?
no, I am in suburbia, in Sour Hill
on a wet autumn afternoon

but I feel confused, wooden minded
like the face of a frightful
yet forgotten deity
on a totem pole in a clearing
my head is wooden, my vision fixed
memories orbit round my brain
sometimes close, sometimes distant
and the fraction of a degree out
could send me hurtling off
in the direction of a God:
there is the sound of a small car in the driveway
I can tell by the noise of its neglected engine
the light beams making circles on the windows
the door slams, footsteps, buzzer
like a mad insect, buzzer
there she goes again –

I am neither sad nor glad
but in my present disposition, indifferent

a small foreign woman, she is voluptuous
and has no scruples massaging my limbs
bringing me to orgasm, which shocked me at first
and she laughed when I told her what she is doing
is considered wrong here, illegal,
'You people,' she shrugged, and continued,
'So many rules and hang-ups and conceits,'

until I am like some perverse child:
she has made it her job
she doesn't count morals, only money
she doesn't pretend she is providing
a social service. a sponsored way
of society ridding itself of the broken and damaged
she smiles, she is only reducing bills

and she has a young lover
who fucks her like he is trying to kill
or anoint, or claim her like the sea
but it only makes her laugh
even Buddha has been reduced
in his infinite wisdom to a hand job.

She smells of cooking
she smells of perfume
her breasts are over-large
like her hips and thighs
she has dark matted hair under her arms
on her legs, bags under her eyes
from too much late night drinking or praying
a fungal infection on none too clean nails

once, she felt sorry for me
and placing me like a log
flat on the floor beneath the window

she flipped me inside her
and rode up and down till I kind of came
and when I started to cry
she stupidly thought it was from gratitude –
I'm not sad she has gone
I'll not miss her in the dark.

There is a helicopter pad
like a small cricket pitch
but I've never seen a helicopter
glide over the lough and trees
and land there, beside the nurses' homes
the prefabricated extensions called Laurel House
Bush House, and so on

the heavy rain that blows in, slant ways
that each of us in our blankets or uniforms
see differently. The full body scan
like modern day archaeologists
looking beneath the dry flaking skin
of a bog woman for kernels of seed
or hair or nail or sex organ

the long needle that numbs the bone
the long needle that draws out the spinal fluid
the dizziness, the prolonged headache
the wad of cotton pad taped like a nappy
to the back, an aged and awkward geisha girl -

what are you saying?
I want to sit in the waiting room
with its cancer prevention posters
and the helpline phone numbers
that no one will use
the vending machines

with oversized bags of crisps
and bottles of coke
as though we were children needing comforting
the girl with the bald head and the coloured nails
the old man with the killing leukaemia
the frightened husband who hates taking a day off
from the building-site –
no one can reach us now
it's all up and over with –

what are you saying?
will you go out tonight?
In your make-up and dress of make believe
and tension, bigger than the worries
or stress of work
yes, I know what you are saying
that banalities won't save me now
or pleasure, or travel, or poems
that I am and yet am no longer
a part of the human universe
a soon to be shadow
a non-existent helicopter
the progressive decay of the world.

It is Saturday evening again,
I'm sure of it now
the pain has gone, the emotion has gone
like the fear of a bull in the ring
or an acrobat who has finally landed
there are the curtains open on a Sour Hill night
the streetlights are now lifeless to me
I hear rain, but have no understanding of rain
or feeling, or sensation
I am neither sad nor happy nor angry
nor afraid, nor expectant

but feel dry like a small leaf
caught in a spider web
between the hedgerows of a lane
leading down to the golf club
soon to be gusted away for good.

There is a great ambience of freedom
and release, like a difficult poem
finished and discarded and unread

a blue light forms around this bubble
a skin-tight bubble that is lighter than air
or life itself, floating
oscillating above the husk that is a man
a silly, awkward shape on the carpet
like the intimate part that rests
in her hand for a while and is gone.

10 THE PUPPET MASTERS

Hotel on a Frozen Beach

After a while you become used
to what once would have been thought absurd –
there are no boundaries or limits anymore
as if someone divine had taken every measure
by which men gauge time and calendar divisions
lunar and natural seasons, the tense-scape of the mind
and jumbled them all together
so that we are left with a presence
that is somewhat familiar
but out of normal sync:

this hotel sits on a frozen beach
the waves of this snottery sea
are frozen thinly at the fringes
it could be the North Sea
it could be farther North
there are high manmade dunes
and the sense of a frontier
from which no one will venture inland
from which no one will sail out from

people walk slowly up and down the strand
but never meet, are always at a shady distance
so that one can't quite make out their clothes
or features – some have children or what appears
to be little dogs running round them in circles
like dust devils

the hotel is always seen at a distance
out of perspective with the horizon
but to enter its echoing hall
you have to *think* yourself in it
the squat wooden building with old wallpaper
surrounding verandas, Dutch sloping roof –
it could be a Nazi brothel for officers
or a sanatorium, or asylum
where thin white women of an indiscriminate age
colour-in picture books
take sea-salt baths
are brought to orgasm by fatherly men in white coats
who open them up with wooden spatulas
who massage them with finger and thumb

the windows are opaque, as if there is always a storm
raging outside, sometimes it feels

like everything is topsy-turvy
inside a snow shaker

the man in the hospital bed is dying again
he is crying into the ward
like a low wind I heard once
at a crossroads in rural Alsace
then he becomes calm
his attention and cancer caught
by an invisible something
in the corner of the ceiling –
he turns his head and knowingly winks.

In the attic room without windows
strange smooth manikins in great number
dangle from the roof beams
a forest of swinging bodies
I push my way through
to a day-room of naked figures
with almost Sinaean faces
who masturbate vigorously
the way they were shown by a sex carer.

In the bare yard
they are burying men standing-up
supervised by men in blue hats
who point out each interment:
in this room an old phonograph record
scratches over and over,
You're a fiery wee man, Peter Ballantine.

A cold fog blows in from the sea islands
cutting to the bone, thick and choking
like yellow mustard gas
blowing chip papers into doorways

piling sand along the promenade
in the near distance, the Christian Endeavour building
rises skeletal like a haunted house
its neat spare dormitories
where young men sleep
its functional reading rooms
where young men meet to listen to elders

to read Protestant bibles
to kiss and caress and jerk each other off
and become too strictured
to use the toilets comfortably
who wet their bed sheets with strange dreams
the screams of orgasms and penetration
from the helter-skelter
the hands down trousers
in the ghost train darkness
the macabre laughter of the encased
laughing sailor

send your sisters on to the sands
to hand out tracts
to be offended by donkey erections
who are already dry and brittle and dead
their openings sewed up
with fear of love
other than the exacting love between the thin pages
of the King James
all day silent reading of the scriptures
in preparation for a world to come
that has already came and went:

when my younger aunt's husband
started an affair

the older religious aunt
followed them down to the seaside
a God fearing evangelist on a Sunday train
she narrowed them down to a greasy spoon
and lifting the heavy glass ashtray
from the Formica table
with its half-eaten chips
salt and pepper pots, cracked delft cups
of stewed tea,
she swore a rightful God's vengeance
and smashed it down upon his temple
thick blood pouring from an open wound
onto the threadbare tablecloth

so I know what I'm talking about –
religion here among the natives
is no abstract philosophising
or studied learning
or moral instruction
but an on-going living war
between good and evil
that sometimes crosses over in confusion
but is never doubtful, never wrong
and always just.

This darkness holds me in fear
the popping gas mantles
the creaking floor boards
the wasted time
the waste of boredom
the phantasmagoria that thins to a meaningless point,
then nothing.

The Mechanic

One day, I'll die, like a fly
on a café's dirty window pane,
and was never there, a black and white analogue
backward walk through a senseless life
a straight-backed woman on a horse:

look at those I have destroyed, as I have built
for I have been a builder from the very start

my little Lego and Meccano sets
sand castles on the cold Magilligan strand
afternoon fortresses looking across to Donegal

and car engines, holed carburettors
punctured radiators
the good well-wired hands of a mechanic
or a meat chopper
neither did I drink, or rant and rave
like some I know
a pioneer, in every sense of the word

and as you rise, you find yourself looking down
on squares of fields, factories, and market towns
loughs, rivers, mountains, forests
lone beaches and tower blocks
and public schools
and like God you count on your fingers
all the places that barred admittance
either physical or metaphysical
the missing lexicons from an Ulster dictionary

so something had to give
some spark that sets the engine turning over

is the flame to blame?
yet after all, I set it right again, in the end

it's the space between I can't amend
the old aunts with the shot-away faces
and like every addict, I wake for hours
counting the breaths in the room's darkness

God will forgive, scars cover wounds
and time blurs memories, then dies altogether
like those who were left behind
and all that's left beyond dry text books
from American universities
old news reels, are senseless histories
like personal data printed on a child's mind

the sunny morning, the blue hills and thistle down
of a boy tumbling from the cloudless sky
spinning like an old cylinder motorcycle
into the air, the rotating wheel
the barrel bore of a gun
the coiled wires of a detonator
the green flaked rooms of police barracks
and holding centres
the dead weight of boots and sleep deprivation
the taste of blood, landing on his Bogside
must have inspired something.

Look stranger, my GAA medals, my pioneer pin
the wooden pew I round my arse in
Sour Hill? I never made a visit there
our paths never crossed, but grow there
and in another era, I would have shared
bread and cordial and seeded cake
like any good country neighbour.

And the wind breaks against the windowpane
as the dried out skeletons of small birds
shift and settle in the boarded-up flue
and ships sail along dark shores
and mail trains cross an Ireland of the mind
too much time
too long the hours
to make-believe or jumble things
to explain or deny

the faces I see, I don't recognise
but they are real for all that
I feel their weight upon my closed eyes –
remember the Corgi Club?
I wasn't there, but still I see
these melting faces that seem so ordinary
in their new hair-do's and suits
they could be uncles, aunts, the unborn
their yellow viscous fat grease blocking the drains
those limbless dotted like cows in the rain
the bubbling black seething mass
of sinew, bone, flesh
shovelled up and scooped into black bin bags –
give thanks all to me!

I, the mechanic, know how
to put such things together again
as good as new, a smidgeon
of American pie, John Wayne, The Quiet Man
Hibernian Clubs in Hell's Kitchen
(avoid auld mother Auden)
the oldest Irish bar in San Fran
(don't call it that to the locals,
such sensitive, good-living, green people)
a pompom and tickertape parade on 5th Avenue

the plough and stars, Ned Kelly, U2
I've raised man again better than dust
In the White House I trust.

The Dockers

1st docker – I buy my Caterpillar's
on the internet
withstand oil and fire and hazardous chemicals
steel toecaps for falling spanners and putting into holes
just as the training manual said they would
a man of the world, I live in the world
of trade centres and turbine jumbos
squeezed toothpaste, pension plans
multi-nationals, pipe lines, and ritual beheadings
why, I even speak a few words of Polish
I have Catholic friends with whom I drink in neutral places
who understand as I understand
that the world sings to a new hymn sheet
with weekend breaks in Amsterdam
we ogle half-clad Eastern European girls
in red lit windows – why not? the brochures say it's a tourist sight
and company trips to Dublin now
in posh hotels and rugby grounds – none of your blarney now
and there are laws, you know what I mean
my children rise and get degrees
from English universities
and live in suburban housing sprawls
with en suite bathrooms
electric showers, flat screen TVs
recreational cocaine, I love my sport
I now watch GAA games on the Sunday BBC.

2nd docker – Do you think the world will ever end?
like zero-hour contracts

and the minimum wage?
the G8 summit, the Russian game?
the border with so many bridges now –
it simply isn't there
and buildings are coming down in every street
the bombs simply didn't do a good enough job
and slit eyes stare from venetian blinds
in oriental restaurants along the golden mile
illegal immigrants, wage slaves, sex slaves
gone are the shipyards, the idle hands
of Samson and Goliath hanging down
we build oil platforms now and wind turbines
and snigger at how quaint things used to be
like two channels, and Ulster TV
and men in shabby suits on street corners
with primitive backfiring revolvers
and wartime carbines
fighting over barricades and old wounds
now we are free from prejudice and old beliefs
the bandages have fallen from our eyes
like naughty children we bow our heads in shame
and understand the simple complexity of our game
to steam-clean history and begin again
and marry girls who go to the gym
shopping-trips in New York with flights from Belfast, now we're safe
who spin their bodies in walk-in tanning machines
like chicken on fish & chip shop spits
who know all about sexual positions and G-spots and disease
from the internet and daytime TV, and follow Love & Hate on RTE
same-sex marriages
country secluded escort services
in conservative towns like Ballymena, Larne, and Carrickfergus
and marching bands taking
selfies with digital cameras

the face of big brother has a unisex hairdo
but is still red cheeked and farms upcountry.

3rd docker – You have to be careful coming home at night
they look for stragglers
and punch you from the back.
I stay close now, behind my own lines
Ice Cold Harp beer
in an old man's local. I
rent this house, old terrace, cold
and damp, but everything else
is too pricey or taken over
by immigrants who get council
grants and don't work and
have large families and don't
speak the language and breed
like rats. Every other weekend
Liz brings the children round
and we go to the park, hang
about on the swings. Overtime
putting in heating and ventilation
ducts, but I've never enough.
Nights, I go down to the
front, throw stones and
bottles and paint bombs
and golf balls, why not?
they started it, smashing
the old people's windows,
and anyway, it's my flag
and country – isn't it?

4th docker – everyone
goes away anyway, nowhere
is big enough, or cosmopolitan
enough over here. When I

moved to the city after
years of commuting from
the country

I thought I had made a
significant change
but things are the same
for the soul is hungry for
that different *something*

and each time I breathe in
fire, I look up at the same
clouds and feel like that
white faced man hanging
by his fingertips to the
clock face

pray for us, the old Gods of
the small ways, who know us
always, and sing, for the
molecule chain of living that
was always there when
first we feared to breathe air
and then the fear of never
breathing again.

Eternity is the boredom of
a wet Sunday behind curtains
and old programmes on the TV
and monotonous sex in half dark
bedrooms, like old poets
stuffed to the gizzard
with windy words
in locked museums.

Oh Lord, show me how to
prime a bomb, to assemble a rifle
load an automatic pistol
for my arse is sodden
standing against a bare
tree in the Bois de Boulogne
getting sucked off by a foreign whore
and mother of three, who might
just be a man –
and they call this life.

How far we have come
crawling out of the alluvial
mud, all blinking eyes
of wonderment, and sac lined
lungs gasping for the first
breath, and limbs and sucker
mouths flailing and
biting over one another in
our race to the land

under a grey sky and a
shore of rocks and boulders, how amazed
we must have been!
a whole land and millenniums
to call and stake as our own:
the God that made us from the
dust, must have wondered
how creation came to this.

11 EPILOGUE: THE POEM BEGINS

The Sour Hill is angry –
all night the storm raged
from the hinterland of the extinct volcano
howling in the crevices of huddled houses
gate posts, hedges, the dried out husks of rotten trees

leaves, multi-coloured, blowing like a snow shower
across the gardens
the waters of the dark river foaming and cresting
downstream to the main watercourse

and in the morning, the dark morning, the first morning
we pick up where we left off a million times
a piece of earth, molten lava
spat-up and left to cool
grown upon, trod upon, built on
cultivated, tamed, fought over
to come

to this
tame as a puppy's tail
milkmen going from gate to gate
soon to be extinct themselves
postmen, now so late they could be from yesterday
delivery lorries up and down the road
school children unaware of the future
pensioners, without a future
but buying the newspapers anyway –

all day, they cross and recross
each pathway of personal history
what does it all mean?
what is it all for?

as useless as the second rate statue
of Armed Science in the public park

or the snaking funeral out to the new graveyard
or an old terrorist plot
that is now a new terrorist plot
or a foreign woman with a Lidl bag
of hand creams and oils
getting into her little car
and thinking it is normal

the silver toy planes waking across the sky
where passengers, looking down,
imagine they can see detail
while dog walkers and workers looking up
imagine they see rows of Godly faces.

Speed it all up, rev it up
and what do you see?
repetition, the maelstrom of the world
shaken up like the glass globe of a snow shaker.

This dark earth will swallow everyone and everything
in the end, down to the white roots and bone
and we will all be dead
consecrated like church ground
by the transfiguration of existence.

It is getting late now, and nothing much has happened
the schoolchildren home to TV and laptops
the afternoon lovers sated and guilty
the old fearing the evening
and the closing of the blinds

the light is leaving a fierce sky from the West
bits of irregular cloud blowing like pieces of torn flag
the last of the golfers are hanging on to the green
playing a last ball before the coming of the dark
Sir Faithful Fortescue is still a rebel
looking for a hole in the sky
so that he can step through
and back to a long gone beginning

the nightshift is starting
with cups of black coffee that are common now
as they watch the last of the civil servants
leave the building

the impeccably dressed grey men
are already gathering near the small bridge
where it becomes darkest
where there are no spotlights or infrared cameras

and the narrator's ghost tries
still, to make sense of his predicament
tries but fails to walk through a hidden wall
bounded by a road and hill

while these two take the opportunity
to set up their recording equipment
in the thick part of the wood
and record the night wind blowing over like migrating souls
the stream, the horrible caw-caw of the hundreds of crows
returning from the surrounding fields
and gathering on the tree tops
as they have always done

as everything will come round again
repeat itself endlessly

the same leaves falling
the same rain and wind
the same habitual ghosts
the same old tired universe.

Sour Hill is a book-length poem set in the town land of Sour Hill in County Antrim. It tells the story of a rural area fast becoming urbanised, through the different peoples who have invaded, settled, lived and died there, through their personal and shared histories – the Viking raids, the Moravians, Irish war of independence, the 'troubles' and the present. Also the more individual, idiosyncratic lives of those who have been damaged or corrupted by their lives. The ghosts who still haunt old houses and woods that had long since disappeared, the Irish servant girls, the hypocrisies of the different churches, preaching about God, but whose congregations act very differently in private.
the builders and architects who cleared the land and built public buildings and suburban houses. Ultimately, the indestructability of the land, and of live itself.